Imam Ali (AS)
The Lion of Allah

Colouring and Activity Book

Fasiha Zehara

In the name of Allah, The Most
Merciful and Beneficent.

The Birth Of Imam Ali (AS)

Imam Ali (AS) was born inside the Holy kaaba in Mecca on the 13th of Rajab, 600 AD. His parents were Abu Talib ibn Abdul Muttalib and Fatima binte Asad.

Imam Ali (AS) did not open his eyes for 3 days. On the fourth day the Holy Prophet (SWS) received Imam Ali (AS) in his arms and He recited azan and iqamah in the child's ears and named him 'Ali' after receiving instructions from Allah through Angel Jibraeel.

The Birth Of Imam Ali (AS)

Battle of Uhad

The Battle of Uhud was the second battle the Muslims fought against the disbelievers. Imam Ali (AS) was the flag-bearer of the Muslim army and he and Hazrat Hamza killed many enemies bravely. Victory was very close, but some Muslim warriors ran away from the battlefield and the disbelievers attacked the Muslims from behind. This mistake and greed of a few Muslims caused them heavy losses.

Many were killed and the Holy Prophet (SWS) was wounded. Imam Ali (AS) fought bravely and He defended the Holy Prophet (SWS) and Islam in such a gallant manner that angel Jibraeel said:

**"There is no warrior but Ali.
There is no sword but Zulfiqar"**

The Battle Of Uhud

The Battle Of Khaibar

Battle of Khaibar was one of the greatest battles fought between Jews and Muslims.
Imam Ali (AS), the greatest warrior, the hero of Islam came to the battlefield with his Zulfiqar to conquer the Jews.

Marhab, a renowned strong Jew warrior, came forward and said "I am Marhab. I dive into my weapons and I attack in a daring way."

Imam Ali (AS) replied, **"I am one whose mother has named him Haider (brave lion). I step into the battlefield with my sword like a ferocious lion, I am lion of jungle, solid and hard"**
Then Imam Ali (AS) took his Zulfiqar and killed Marhab in single strike.

Then he at once pulled out a part of the gate of **Khaibar**, which 40 strong men used to open and close. It seemed that Allah did not want anyone but Ali (AS) to bring victory to Islam.

The Battle Of Khaibar

The Event Of Ghadeer

On the 18th of Dhul Hijjah of the year 10 AH, Prophet Muhammad (SWS) upon returning from the farewell Hajj stopped in Ghadeer Khumm, assembled the Muslims and The Messenger of Allah (SWS) declared:
"I am leaving for you two precious things and if you adhere to them both, you will never go astray after me. They are the Book of Allah (Qur'an) and my Progeny, that is my Ahlul Bayt. The two shall never separate from each other until they come to me by the Pool of Kausar."

The Prophet (SWS) held up the hand of Ali (AS) and said:
"For whoever I am his Leader (Mawla),
Ali is his Leader (Mawla)."

Immediately after the Prophet (SWS) finished his speech, the following verse of the Qur'an was revealed:
"Today I have perfected your religion and completed my favour upon you, and I was satisfied that Islam be your religion." (Qur'an 5:3)

Imam Sadiq (AS) said:
Eid-e-Ghadeer is the greatest Eid of Allah (swt)

The Event Of Ghadeer

Zakat (Charity)

Imam Ali (AS) gave his ring as zakat to a beggar in the position of Rukoo, while praying 'Salaat'. All the companions were praying behind the Holy Prophet (SWS). The beggar came in and asked for charity. No one paid any attention. Being disappointed, he was going away. At that moment Imam Ali (AS) held out his hand, The beggar saw and took the ring.

Then the verse of the Quran came down "Verily your 'Walee' is Allah; and His Messenger and those who establish 'Salaat', and pay 'Zakaat' while they be in 'Rukoo'. (Surah Al-Maidah, Verse 55) "

Zakat (Charity)

FATHER OF ORPHAN

Imam Ali (AS) attached great importance to orphans, and he used to caress them. He would say, "I am the father of the orphans. I must show compassion to them, so that I will have treated them like a father." Muslims of that time used to say, "I had wished I was an orphan too, so that I would have received the same attention and kindness from the Commander of the Faithful (AS)."

The Holy Prophet (SWS) has spoken about the virtue, wisdom and mercy of Imam Ali (AS) in many hadiths.

Among the hadiths, we can mention the hadith: (يا علي أنا وأنت أبوا هذه الامة) that the Prophet himself and Imam Ali (AS) have been called the **fathers of this ummah**.

Father Of The Orphans

MARTYRDOM OF ALI (AS)

In the morning of 19th Shahr Ramadan, 40 AH, Imam Ali (AS) was praying with his followers in Masjid e Kufa, at that time Ibn Maljum struck Imam Ali's (AS) head with a poisoned sword. He died on the 21st Shahr Ramadan, 40 AH and buried in the city of Najaf.

He was born in the House of Allah, the Kaaba, and martyred in the House of Allah, Masjid al-Kufa.

The Lion of Allah, the most brave and gentle Muslim after the Prophet (SWS) himself, began his glorious life with devotion to Allah and His Messenger, and ended it in the service of Islam.

Martyrdom Of Ali (AS)

Shrine Of Imam Ali (AS)

Shrine of Imam Ali (AS) is located in the city of Najaf, Iraq and is the place where he has been buried. For nearly hundred years after his demise, the location of his grave was a secret. Imam Sadiq (AS) revealed the burial place of the Imam in 135 AH. After that, different buildings were built on this tomb at different times. Millions of Muslims from all over the world come every year to this shrine to offer salutation and to pray to Allah seeking his intercession and to kiss the dhari of the tomb of the Imam Ali (AS). Those who cannot afford to go there personally, are constantly praying to Allah to help them to visit the shrine of their Maula Ali (AS), and others request to offer salutations on their behalf, and to pray to God for some particular favour and to seek Imam Ali's intercession and to say Labbaik to Imam Ali (AS).

Shrine Of Imam Ali (AS)

Activities

Search the Famous Titles of Imam Ali (AS)

```
L D H A B U T U R A B F K U S A W V
I M A M U L M U T T A Q E E N B Z H
Z Z F A S A D U L L A H Y G G U F O
R D M Y R Q M Q Y B V U D D K L H T
A I N U L L A H L U I K C B H H A L
N L M A Z H A R U L A J A I B A B I
A E R G H A I D A R V Z A N V S X E
J S A I F U L L A H U A Q U V A V F
S L X E P W J I F S Q Y O D S N T M
W V Y D H V E G W A L I U L L A H J
A M E E R A L M O M I N E E N U C A
T M N R X E Q Y M U R T A Z A P O Q
```

Find the following words in the puzzle.
Words are hidden → ↓ and ↘ .

ABULHASAN

ABUTURAB

AINULLAH

AMEERALMOMINEEN

ASADULLAH

HAIDAR

IMAMULMUTTAQEEN

MAZHARULAJAIB

MURTAZA

SAIFULLAH

WALIULLAH

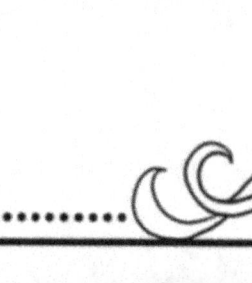

Connect the dots

Imam Ali (AS) is called the Lion of Allah

Spot the Differences

Imam Ali (AS) Quiz

Choose the right answer:

1. Which is the birthplace of Imam Ali (AS)?
   a) Medina   b) Karbala   c) Mecca (Kaaba)

2. In which battle did Imam Ali (AS) get the Zulfiqar?
   a) Uhad   b) Khaibar   c) Badr

3. When did Prophet Mohammed (SWS) made
   Imam Ali (AS) the leader?
   a) Mubahilla   b) Ghadeer   c) Battle of Uhad

4. What Zakat did Imam Ali (AS) give in Ruku?
   a) Money   b) Ring   c) Clothes

5. In which month did Imam Ali (AS) was martyred?
   a) Shahr Ramadan   b) Muharram   c) Shabaan

6. Where is the shrine of Imam Ali (AS)?
   a) Karbala   b) Medina   c) Najaf

Find your Path to Imam Ali (AS)

You're here

www.ingramcontent.com/pod-product-compliance
Lightning Source LLC
Chambersburg PA
CBHW080853120626
46546CB00009B/2805